God's Word:
Alive And Active

Eight Children's Sermons
And Activity Pages

Julia E. Bland

CSS Publishing Company, Inc., Lima, Ohio

Dedicated to
Paul, teacher of teachers.

Copyright © 2002 by
CSS Publishing Company, Inc.
Lima, Ohio

For more information about CSS Publishing Company resources, visit our website at www.csspub.com or e-mail us at custserv@csspub.com or call (800) 241-4056.

ISBN: 0-7880-1954-6

Table Of Contents

Introduction And Suggestions From The Author

It is important for children as well as adults to be reminded of how precious and vital the word of God is. This is the purpose of these lessons.

Study each sermon so that you can tell it in your own words, using your own personality and keeping the needs of your local children in mind.

The sermon as given is to get you started. Be open to the Holy Spirit as he guides you to add your own personal observations.

If you need notes, make them small and tuck them inside your Bible at the pages where you will be reading the Scripture. Open the Bible and read from it. Children need to know that what you say really is from the Scriptures.

Ask questions and allow time for the children to answer. This will get them thinking and involved, but children can say unexpected things, so be ready to guide them back to the subject.

Before the worship hour, clip the activity sheet, a pencil, and crayons to a clipboard to be ready to hand to each child when the children's time is over.

These lessons have been prepared with the morning worship hour in mind, but they may be used any time there is opportunity for Christian education of children.

As you pray and prepare, claim the Lord's promise in Isaiah 55:11:

So shall my word be that goes out from my mouth;
it shall not return to me empty,
but it shall accomplish that which I purpose,
and succeed in the thing for which I sent it.

God bless you as you teach our children.

Julia E. Bland

God's Word Is Real

... The ordinances of the Lord are true and righteous altogether. (Psalm 19:9b)

Scripture: 2 Peter 1:16, 21; also see 2 Timothy 3:16

Visual Aids: Bible and children's storybook

Handouts: Activity sheets

Advance Preparations: Copy enough activity pages for each child to have one.

The Sermon:

I have a *storybook. Do you like to have Mom or Dad or someone read you stories? Or maybe you can read them yourself. What kind do you like? There are lots of fun stories like "The Three Bears," "The Three Pigs," and "Peter Rabbit." Or maybe you like *The Jungle Book*, *Bambi*, or *The Wizard of Oz*.

What is the difference between those stories and the stories in the *Bible? Those stories are only make-believe. They didn't really happen. They are called fiction. Here is my *Bible and the stories in it are real. Listen to this from the Bible in 2 Peter 1:16: "For we did not follow cleverly devised myths when we made known to you the power and coming of our Lord Jesus Christ, but we had been eyewitnesses of his majesty."

Peter was a friend and disciple of Jesus. He says he did not make up the stories about Jesus, but was with Jesus and saw Jesus with his own eyes and what he tells us about Jesus is real. Then Peter says in verse 21 that it is by God's Holy Spirit that those who gave us God's Word did so. The *Bible, God's Word, is from God!

How did all this happen? The word "Bible" is not used in the Bible. It is called "Scriptures" or "the Word of God." The word "Bible" is a Latin word that means "little books." There are 66 of these little books. It took over 1,000 years for all the little books to be written and put together.

God called all kinds of people to write the books. They were lawgivers, soldiers, wise men, prophets, kings, priests, fishermen, poets, storytellers, farmers, officials, physicians, and missionaries. They were all kinds of people, but they all knew God and listened to him and wrote down what he said and did.

Only by God's guidance could a book be written by so many people taking so many years and still all fit together so well.

The Bible was first written not in English, but in other languages — Hebrew and Greek. In those days hundreds of years ago, all Scripture was written by hand on rolls of animal skin called parchment or on papyrus which was made from a water plant. Those rolls are called scrolls and they were in use when Jesus lived. Today we have paper and printing presses, copiers, and computers.

The Bible has had enemies. When people first started to put God's Word into languages that all could understand, there were many who did not approve. Those who did this work suffered and some were killed. In some countries it has been against the law to print or own a Bible. People have suffered and died to preserve the Bible. So it is a very precious book. It has outlived and outsold all other books.

We know the *Bible is real and comes from God. That is why we read it and hear it taught. I'm glad you are here today for that purpose.

*Use visual aids

God's Word Is Like A Foundation

Happy are those who keep his decrees.... (Psalm 119:2a)

Scripture: Matthew 7:24-27

Visual Aids: Bible and the story folder

Handouts: Activity sheets and story folders (story folder on page 35)

Advance Preparations: Copy enough activity pages and story folders for each child to have one. Fold the story page in half the long way so that page 1 is at the bottom right corner. Fold again the other way. The story will then have pages 1 through 4 in order. Be ready to use the folder with the children as you tell the story.

The Sermon:
Last time we were together we talked about the *Bible and other kinds of books. Some stories are made up. They are lots of fun, but they are not true. The *Bible and its stories are real. They are true stories and lessons given to us by God.

Jesus said that his word in our *Bible is like a foundation to build our lives upon. We read and hear what God has said. Then we try hard to do it. We build a good, strong, happy life when we listen and do what he said in our Bible.

Here is a *folder with something Jesus said in Matthew 7:24-27. There on page 1 is a house. Do you see the foundation? The foundation is that rock at the bottom. Let's read on page 1 what Jesus said: "Everyone then who hears these words of mine and acts on them will be like a wise man who built his house on rock."

And page 2 says: "The rain fell, the floods came, and the winds blew and beat on that house, but it did not fall because it had been founded on rock."

Jesus means that we should listen to what he has said and do as he asks, then our lives will be strong, like a house on a rock foundation. And if trouble or problems come to us, these stormy times will not really hurt or destroy us because we trust in Jesus for all the help we need.

Now page 3 says: "And everyone who hears these words of mine and does not act on them will be like a foolish man who built his house on sand." Look at that house. It has no foundation of rock. So what happens?

Page 4 says: "The rain fell, and the floods came, and the winds blew and beat against that house, and it fell — and great was its fall!"

Jesus means that if we don't listen to what he has said and don't do as he asks, then our lives will be weak like the house without a foundation. When we have problems or trouble and stormy times, our lives will suffer. We have no one to turn to for the help we need and we will be like the house that fell and was destroyed in the storm.

We want a strong, happy life. Let's hear what Jesus says and try to do as he teaches.

*Use visual aids

God's Word Is Like A Map

This is the way; walk in it. (Isaiah 30:21b)

Scripture: John 14:6; Psalm 23:3b; Proverbs 15:24a

Visual Aids: Bible and a map

Handouts: Activity sheets

Advance Preparations: Copy enough activity pages for each child to have one. Find a place on the map to visit and be prepared to show the children the road you would take to get there.

The Sermon:

Have you ever taken a trip? What is one important thing that you will need to tell you how to get there? A *map, of course. Maps show the way to go. We must take the right road to get where we want. *If I want to go to _____, then here is the road I must take. Maps also tell interesting things about where we are going and places along the way to help us enjoy our trip.

The Bible speaks of walking paths as though living our life is like a journey. Listen to Proverbs 15:24a: "For the wise the path of life leads upward...." And Psalm 23:3b says: "He (God) leads me in right paths for his name's sake."

If living life is like a journey along a path, then the *Bible is like a map. The Bible tells us the way to go. It tells us Jesus is the way. John 14:6 says: "Jesus said to him, 'I am the way, and the truth, and the life. No one comes to the Father except through me.' "

So, we must start off trusting Jesus. Then the *Bible is like a map giving directions. Jesus helps us understand and follow the directions. We must trust Jesus and follow the directions or we'll never get there. Where? To heaven, of course. We all want to go to heaven, but we want a happy life, a happy journey as we go.

The *Bible tells us all we need to know to have this happy life-journey. That is why it is so important for you to come to church and Sunday school and hear what the Bible has to say. We need to read our Bible at home, too. Then, most important of all, we need to do what it says.

*Use visual aids

God's Word Is Like Seed

I treasure your word in my heart.... (Psalm 119:11a)

Scripture: Matthew 13:3-8, 18-23; Galatians 5:22

Visual Aids: Bible and story folder

Handouts: Activity sheets and story folders (story folder on page 37)

Advance Preparations: Copy enough activity pages and story folders for each child to have one. Fold the story folder in half the long way so that page 1 is at the bottom right corner. Fold again the other way. The story will then have pages 1 through 4 in order. Be ready to use the folder with the children as you tell the story.

The Sermon:

We have been learning some things about God's word in our *Bible. We know God's word is real and true and that it is like a foundation to build our lives on. God's word is also like a map showing us the way to go as we live this life.

One day, Jesus told his disciples that the word of God is like seed. Jesus told them a story that we call a parable. Parables are stories that use common ordinary things that everyone knows about to help us understand some things God wants us to know. Everyone knows what seeds are and that they should be planted. In this story a man went out to plant seeds. There were no machines in those days, so it was done all by hand.

Let's look at *page 1 of this story. So Jesus said, "Some seeds fell on the path, and the birds came and ate them up." The birds are having a good treat, aren't they?

Now let's look at *pages 2 and 3. "Other seeds fell on rocky ground ... and since they had no roots, they withered away." Why didn't they have roots? Is it because the rock was in the way?

The next verse says, "Other seeds fell among thorns, and the thorns grew up and choked them." These plants could not grow because the weeds and thorns crowded them all out.

But look at the last picture on *page 3. "Other seeds fell on good soil and brought forth grain." The disciples had heard the story, but they did not understand what Jesus meant. So Jesus explained.

Let's look at *page 1 again. Jesus told them that the seed stands for God's word. The seed that fell on the path is like God's word in a person's heart, but the Devil comes and takes it away. The heart of that person never believes, never trusts Jesus as their Lord.

Look at *pages 2 and 3. Jesus told them that the seed on the rocky ground stands for God's word in a heart that does not let it sink in, so that after a while when they have trouble of some sort they do not remain in their faith. And the seed that fell into thorns and weeds stands for God's word in hearts that are full of other things, like getting rich or being famous, so that God's word gets crowded out of their life.

But Jesus said some seed fell in good ground and grew. Now, let's look at *page 4. "But as for what was sown on good soil, this is the one who hears the word and understands it, who indeed bears fruit."

Jesus is saying that the seed in good ground is like God's word in a heart that receives it, believes it, and lets it sink deep into their life. They become good, strong Christians and the seed of God's word produces a lot of good things. What are these good things? Galatians 5:22 tells us: "... love, joy, peace, patience, kindness, generosity, faithfulness, gentleness, and self-control."

These are the kinds of things that make for a happy life. Let's open our hearts to God's word, take Jesus as our Savior, and live the life that is happy. (Did you find some hidden hearts in our folder?)

*Use visual aids

God's Word Is Like A Mirror

... The commandment of the Lord is clear, enlightening the eyes. (Psalm 19:8b)

Scripture: James 1:23-25; 2:8b; 4:11

Visual Aids: Bible and hand mirror

Handouts: Activity sheets

Advance Preparations: Copy enough activity pages for each child to have one.

The Sermon:

We've been talking about God's word that is here in our *Bible. God's word is real and true. It is like a foundation to build our lives upon. It is like a map showing us the way to live a happy life on our way to heaven by trusting in Jesus and doing the things he says. Jesus said his word is like seeds planted in good soil, and he meant our heart was like good soil so that when we listen to his word and obey, we will produce a crop of all kinds of good things like love, joy, and peace.

So today, let's talk about God's word again. Here is a *mirror. Suppose you look in the *mirror and see dirt on your face, perhaps a ring of Kool-Aid or chocolate around your mouth. Or perhaps you see messy hair. What will you do? You will wash your face or comb your hair. It would be stupid to look and see what you need and yet not do anything about it.

The *Bible says God's word is like a *mirror. We can look in the Bible, reading what it says, and see ourselves in what we read, and realize that something needs to be changed. When we look in a mirror, we see ourselves and not someone else. We look at ourselves and see what *we* need.

Let's look right here in the book of James. Chapter 2, verse 8 says, "You shall love your neighbor as yourself." We all know we don't love each other as we should. This is something we see about ourselves that we need to change, to work on, and to do better.

Another verse, James 4:11, says, "Do not speak evil against one another." Again, this is something that we need to do better, and we need to watch what we say.

Some people look, hear, or read God's word but don't do anything about it.

James 1:23-24 says: "For if any are hearers of the word and not doers, they are like those who look at themselves in a mirror, for they look at themselves, and on going away immediately forget what they were like."

Then the last of verse 25 says, "... doers who act — they will be blessed in their doing."

God's word is like a mirror. We see ourselves there and we work with God's help to change and to do better, and the Bible promises we will be blessed — made happy — if we do.

*Use visual aids

God's Word Is Like A Lamp

The unfolding of your words gives light.... (Psalm 119:130a)

Scripture: Psalm 119:105

Visual Aids: Bible and flashlight

Handouts: Activity sheets

Advance Preparations: Copy enough activity pages for each child to have one.

The Sermon:

Do you like the dark? When the sun goes down in the evening, we have to turn on lights. We would stumble or bump into things and maybe fall down if we had no light at night.

Have you ever gone camping? At night it is very dark in places where there is no electricity or lights, so we remember to take along a *flashlight.

The Bible tells us in Psalm 119:105, "Your word is a lamp to my feet and a light to my path."

Now, the Bible is talking about a different kind of darkness. Darkness is bad, evil, sinful things, or things that hurt, or sad, hopeless, unhappy things that happen in our world and in our living. Sunlight does not help this kind of darkness, nor does electricity or a *flashlight. We need a special kind of light.

I'm sorry to say that as long as we live in this world, there will be this darkness of sin and hurt and unhappiness around us. Perhaps we all will have this darkness in our own lives, but God has not wanted it to be this way.

The verse we read tells us God's word in our *Bible is like a lamp or light. God's word tells us how to miss much of the darkness of sin and sorrow. God's word is like a lamp (or *flashlight) that we need on the journey of life. We talked about God's word being like a map and telling us that Jesus is the way to go. God's word is also like a lamp or light showing us how to miss bad things, how not to make hurtful mistakes and stumble on the path of life.

But, if we don't turn the *flashlight on, we won't have light. If we don't read *God's word or hear it taught or do as God has said, it cannot help us.

*Use visual aids

God's Word Is Alive And Eternal

Heaven and earth will pass away, but my words will not pass away. (Matthew 24:35)

Scripture: Hebrews 4:12a; Isaiah 55:11; Isaiah 40:8

Visual Aids: Bible and flower

Handouts: Activity sheets

Advance Preparations: Copy enough activity pages for each child to have one.

The Sermon:

For several weeks we've been thinking and talking about God's word. God's word is real, not made-up stories. It's like a foundation to build our lives on. It's like a map to show us the way to go through life. It's like seeds planted in our hearts to produce a crop of happy things. It's like a mirror that shows us how we can improve and do better. It's like a lamp to light our way so that we don't make bad mistakes and stumble as we live.

Yes, God's word here in our *Bible is really special. There are some other special things about his word. It is alive. Hebrews 4:12 says, "Indeed, the word of God is living and active...."

This means that it does things like change people's lives from bad to good. God's word comforts us if we are sad by telling us how much God loves and wants to help us. God's word gives us hope because he tells us he will forgive us if we do wrong things and that he has prepared a place for us. If we'll trust and love Jesus, heaven will be our home some day. God's word is alive and does things. In Isaiah 55:11 God says his word will accomplish things, "So shall my word be that goes out from my mouth; it shall not return to me empty, but it shall accomplish that which I purpose, and succeed in the thing for which I sent it."

There is something else too that is special. His word will never pass away. What happens to *flowers after they have bloomed? Do their petals turn brown and drop off? Sometimes they are so pretty we wish they'd last forever, but they don't. Listen to Isaiah 40:8, "The grass withers, the flower fades; but the word of our God will stand forever."

God's word is forever. God will keep all his promises. God will not change his mind. If God says he loves you, then you can depend on it. If God says he has prepared us a home in heaven, we can count on it. If God says we must be sorry for our sins and trust in Jesus to forgive us and be our Lord, then that is exactly what we must do.

It is good to know we can depend on God's word. *God's word is special! Let's read it or hear it taught and make it part of our life.

*Use visual aids

God's Word Became A Person Like Us

In the beginning was the Word, and the Word was with God, and the Word was God. (John 1:1)

Scripture: John 1:14; 12:49; 8:12; also see Matthew 7:24; John 14:6; Galatians 5:22; Hebrews 12:2a; John 3:16

Visual Aids: Bible, pictures of Jesus, and the visual aids used in earlier lessons if desired

Handouts: Activity sheets

Advance Preparations: Copy enough activity pages for each child to have one.

The Sermon:

In the Bible we have many names for Jesus. He is called names like Son of God, Savior, Lord, Christ, Master, and Teacher. There is another name for Jesus that maybe you've never heard before. When John wrote about Jesus, he called him the Word. John 1:14 says, "And the Word became flesh and lived among us, and we have seen his glory, the glory as of a father's only son, full of grace and truth."

Let's say it this way — and Jesus *the Word* became flesh and lived among us. "Became flesh" means he became *human. You all know the Christmas story of how God's Son, Jesus, was born a baby, grew up living life as we do, as a *person just like us. First he was a baby, then a boy, and then a man who was a carpenter.

For several weeks we have talked of God's word, the words written here in our *Bible. We have seen how his words can help us with our life by being like a foundation, like a map, like seeds, like a mirror, and like a lamp. We have learned that God's word is alive, active, and will never pass away.

So what can it mean to say Jesus is the Word? I think it means that the life Jesus lived showed us exactly what God's word means. Jesus was God's word in action. Jesus put God's word into action by showing God's love as he lived on earth with his teaching, healing, and help, and then with his dying on a cross to save us. So if we want to understand God's word, we need to look at Jesus, for the life of Jesus makes God's word plain. Jesus said that everything he taught and did was God's word and came from the Heavenly Father. John 12:49 tells us that Jesus said, "For I have not spoken on my own, but the Father who sent me has himself given me a commandment about what to say and what to speak."

So, is Jesus the Word like a *foundation? Yes. In order to have a strong, happy life we need to build our life on Jesus and what he has said (Matthew 7:24).

Is Jesus the Word like a *map? Yes. Jesus said he is the way. We take Jesus as Lord and go the way he teaches on the path of life and to heaven (John 14:6).

Is Jesus the Word like *seeds? Yes. Jesus in our hearts will produce a crop of good things — love, joy, peace, patience, kindness, generosity, faithfulness, gentleness, and self-control (Galatians 5:22).

Is Jesus the Word like a *mirror? Yes. When we look at Jesus and his life and what he taught, we see what we need to do to be better. We don't look at someone else and say, "I'm better than he or she is." We look at Jesus and see how *we* need to improve (Hebrews 12:2a).

Is Jesus the Word like a *lamp? Here's what Jesus said in John 8:12: "I am the light of the world. Whoever follows me will never walk in darkness but will have the light of life." Loving and following Jesus gives us light for our life, we will escape the darkness of sin and not stumble making bad mistakes.

And Jesus the Word is alive and active and he will never end or pass away. Jesus is forever. Trusting and loving Jesus gives us life with him that never ends (John 3:16).

What God has done for us is wonderful: we have God's written word here in our *Bible. We can have his word, his presence, in all our life. Let's read our Bible, come to Sunday school and church, and get to know Jesus and his love better.

*Use visual aids

When Jesus lived, God's word was written by hand on scrolls.

Use the list of words below to fill in the blanks.

Some stories are _ _ _ _ _ _ _. That means they didn't really happen. They are make-believe. Some stories are _ _ _ _. That means they are true. The _ _ _ _ _ _ _ and lessons in the Bible are true.

The word *Bible* comes from a Latin word. It _ _ _ _ _ "little books." There are 66 _ _ _ _ _ in our Bible. The Bible is also called Scripture or the Word of God. Earliest Scripture was written on animal _ _ _ _ or papyrus and made into rolls called _ _ _ _ _ _ _. Today we have printing presses, computers, and copiers to use.

Kings, prophets, fishermen, farmers, physicians, and missionaries were _ _ _ _ of those who were _ _ _ _ _ _ by God's Holy Spirit to write. It took over 1,000 _ _ _ _ _ for the Bible to be completed. Only with God's guidance _ _ _ _ _ such a book be written by so _ _ _ _ people and _ _ _ together so well.

Through the years some have _ _ _ _ _ to destroy the Bible. Others have _ _ _ _ to preserve it. In some countries it has been against the _ _ _ to own or _ _ _ _ _ a Bible. To people in those countries, the Bible is _ _ _ _ precious. It should be _ _ _ _ _ _ _ _ _ to _ _ too. We should _ _ _ _ from it each day.

Find words from the list in this word search puzzle. They will go down or left to right.

Y	E	A	R	S	M	A	N	Y	U	S	L
S	F	I	C	T	I	O	N	U	S	C	A
K	A	B	O	O	K	S	T	S	F	R	W
I	C	U	U	R	V	E	R	Y	I	O	R
N	T	S	L	I	P	R	I	N	T	L	E
G	U	I	D	E	D	I	E	D	U	L	A
M	E	A	N	S	U	S	D	X	S	S	D
P	R	E	C	I	O	U	S	S	O	M	E

fiction
means
scrolls
years
fit
law
precious
fact
books
some

could
tried
print
read
stories
skin
guided
many
died
very

us (6 times in word search)

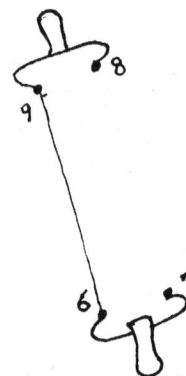

All scripture is inspired by God ...
2 Timothy 3:16a

16

God's Word Is Like A Foundation

Those who hear and do what Jesus says are like a wise man who built his house on rock.

17

Jesus said if we are wise and want a strong, happy life, we need to listen and do what he said. We will be like a house built on rock.

Jesus said that if we do not listen and do as he says, we are like a foolish person who built a house on sand. A storm destroyed that house.

X	H	O	U	S	E	W	H	A	T	R
F	B	U	I	L	T	A	X	N	H	O
O	X	S	T	R	O	N	G	O	A	C
O	H	A	P	P	Y	T	X	T	T	K
L	W	I	S	E	L	I	S	T	E	N
I	X	D	E	S	T	R	O	Y	E	D
S	A	N	D	S	T	O	R	M	D	O
H	L	I	F	E	P	E	R	S	O	N

Here are some words from today's story. Draw a line from each word to what it means.

wise   loose, small grains of rock

strong   a large mass of stone; a firm support

happy   strong wind with rain, thunder and lightning, or snow

listen   to show good judgment

do   to ruin, spoil, tear down, or put an end to

built   to be silly, unwise, or stupid

rock   to put together

foolish   to be powerful; to have special ability

sand   to have joy and be glad

storm   to hear and to take advice

destroyed   to perform or complete

Help this family move to their new house built on a strong foundation.

A map shows us the way to go
on a trip. Jesus and his word
show us the best way to go all
through life.

Jesus said, "I am the way, and the truth, and
the life. No one comes to the father except
through me."   — John 14:6

19

Unscramble the words, then find them in the word search puzzle below.

When we take a trip, maps show us the way to ___. We must take the right _____ to get where we want.
(og) (odra)

_____ also tell interesting things about where we _____ going and places along the way to help us
(apMs) (rea)

_____ our _____. The Bible says that living our _____ is like a journey. If living life is like a
(yojen) (iprt) (feil)

_____ along a _____, then the Bible is like a map. The _____ tells us the way to go. It
(neyurjo) (thpa) (Bbeli)

_____ us Jesus is the way. So we _____ start off trusting Jesus. Then the Bible is like a map giving
(llets) (ustm)

directions. Jesus helps us understand and _____ the _____. We must trust Jesus and
(oowllf) (rectsnoidi)

follow the directions or we'll never _____ _____. Where? To heaven, of course. We all want to go to
(etg) (ereht)

_____, but we want a happy life, a _____ journey as we go.
(veeahn) (pphay)

Use words from Proverbs 15:24 to fill in the squares of this puzzle.

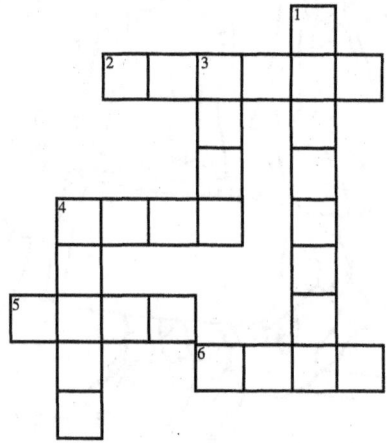

G	F	X	B	P	A	T	H	X	R	G	M
E	O	D	I	R	E	C	T	I	O	N	S
T	L	G	B	E	N	J	O	Y	A	A	L
M	L	O	L	M	T	R	I	P	D	R	I
U	O	H	E	A	V	E	N	G	A	E	F
S	W	H	A	P	P	Y	T	H	E	R	E
T	E	L	L	S	J	O	U	R	N	E	Y

For the wise the path of life leads upward.
Proverbs 15:24

Down
1. Proverbs
3. wise
4. leads

Across
2. upward
4. life
5. path
6. wise

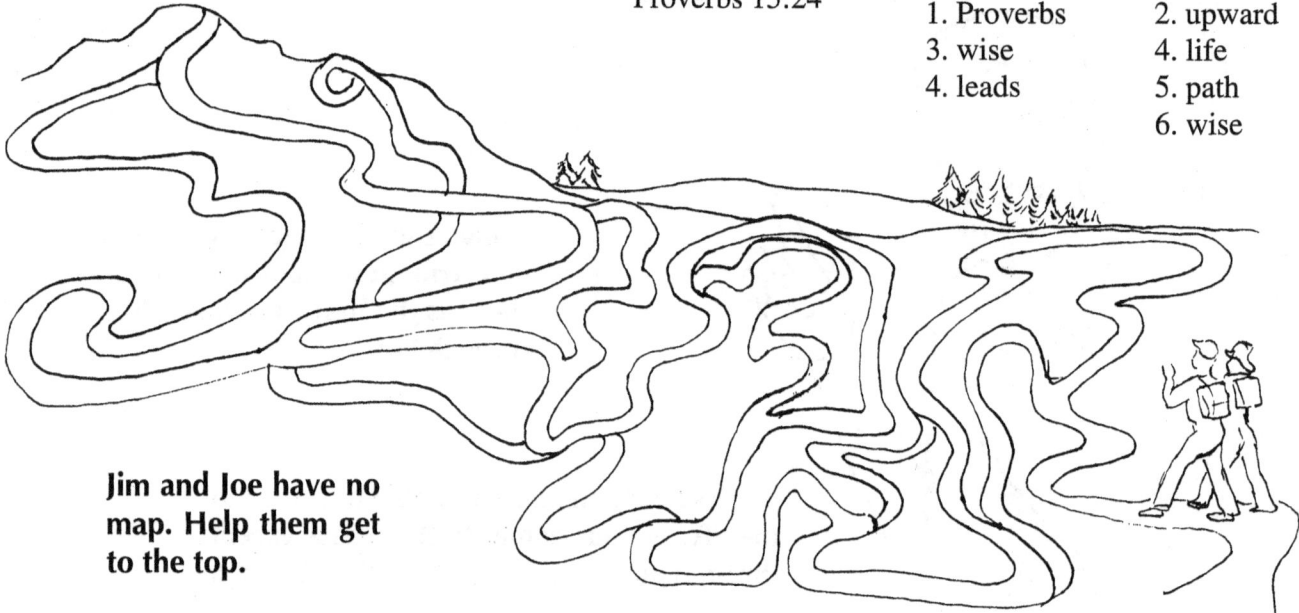

Jim and Joe have no map. Help them get to the top.

Jesus and God's word in our hearts helps us do good things like seeds in good ground make a good crop.

Use the list of words to fill in the blanks.

Jesus told some parables. A _ _ _ _ _ _ _ _ is a story about things everyone

_ _ _ _ _ about. It helps us _ _ _ _ _ _ _ _ _ _ what God means. Jesus told

a parable about _ _ _ _ _ _ _ _ seeds. When seeds fell on the path, _ _ _ _ _

ate them. The seeds on rocky ground had no _ _ _ _ _. Some seed fell among

_ _ _ _ _ _ and the plants were _ _ _ _ _ _ _ out. Some _ _ _ _ fell on

good _ _ _ _ and they grew and produced _ _ _ _ _. The seed stands for God's

_ _ _ _. The soil stands for our _ _ _ _ _. The seed eaten by birds stands for

God's word in hearts that do not _ _ _ _ _ _ _. The seed on rocky ground stands

for God's word in hearts that at first believe but do _ _ _ keep on. The seed in thorny

_ _ _ _ _ _ stands for God's word in hearts that let other things be more important

and God's word gets crowded out. The seed in _ _ _ _ soil stands for God's word in

hearts that believe and _ _ what his word says. The good seed of God's word will

produce a good life. Hearing and doing what God asks gives us happy things like

_ _ _ _, _ _ _, and peace.

parable
understand
roots
soil
heart
ground
love
knows
planting
seed
grain
believe
good
birds
crowded
word
not
thorns
do (3 times
    in puzzle)
joy (3 times
    in puzzle)

Find the words from the list in the puzzle. They will go left to right or down.

J	O	Y	H	E	A	R	T	J	O	Y
P	D	B	S	E	E	D	H	X	S	X
L	O	I	J	O	Y	N	O	T	O	C
A	G	R	A	I	N	X	R	P	I	R
N	R	D	X	X	W	X	N	A	L	O
T	O	S	R	O	O	T	S	R	K	W
I	U	N	D	E	R	S	T	A	N	D
N	N	G	O	O	D	D	O	B	O	E
G	D	L	O	V	E	D	O	L	W	D
X	X	B	E	L	I	E	V	E	S	X

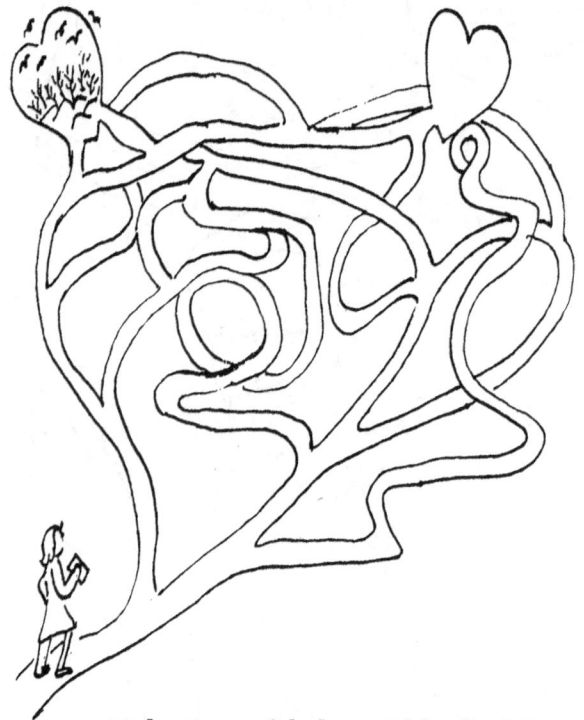

Help Sue with her Bible find her way to the heart that has no birds, rocks, or thorns.

22

God's Word Is Like A Mirror

God's word is like a mirror. It shows us how we can do better.

Find the underlined words in the word search puzzle. They will go left to right or down.

We look in a mirror and see ourselves. Our face is dirty and our hair is messy. So we wash our face and comb our hair. It would be silly to see what we need and just go away not doing anything about it.

The Bible is like a mirror. We read the Bible or hear it taught and we see how we need to do better. We need to do what God's word says. Then we will be blessed or made happy. What are some things you need to do better?

R	F	O	B	S	N	E	E	D	H	W
E	M	O	L	I	N	O	T	I	A	O
A	A	U	E	L	H	A	I	R	P	R
D	D	R	S	L	S	E	E	T	P	D
M	E	S	S	Y	A	W	A	Y	Y	T
I	C	E	E	F	A	C	E	D	E	A
R	O	L	D	D	O	L	O	O	K	U
R	M	V	A	N	Y	T	H	I	N	G
O	B	E	T	T	E	R	X	N	X	H
R	X	S	X	T	H	I	N	G	S	T
W	A	S	H	O	W	E	H	E	A	R

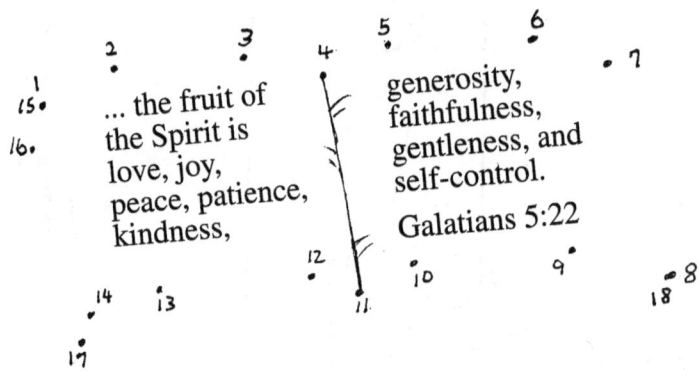

... the fruit of the Spirit is love, joy, peace, patience, kindness, generosity, faithfulness, gentleness, and self-control.

Galatians 5:22

When we look in the Bible at Galatians 5:22, we see some things we need to do better. Draw a line to the words that will finish the sentence.

I show love when I want good t...

I show joy when I s...

I show peace when I try to g...

I show patience when I obey w...

I show kindness when I o...

I show generosity when I s...

I show faithfulness when I k...

I show gentleness when I a...

I show self-control when I r...

I show love for Jesus when I d...

do as he asks.

things for others.

refuse to argue or get angry.

smile.

am careful not to hurt anyone.

share.

offer to help Mom with chores.

without complaining.

get along with others.

keep my promises.

God's word is like a light to help us find our way all through life.

Fill in the missing words. Use the pictures to help.

When the _ _ _ goes down, it is dark. If it is dark, we might stumble or

_ _ _ _ or knock something over. We need to turn on a _ _ _ _ _. The

Bible talks about another kind of darkness. The Bible calls bad, sinful,

<u>u</u> _ <u>h</u> _ _ _ _ things darkness. For this kind of darkness we need a

special kind of light. God's word is that special _ _ _ _ _. God's word

gives us directions on how to live and how to miss a lot of bad, sinful, un-

happy things. We need to do as God's word says. It is like a light showing us

the way to live a happy life.

Find the words from the list in the word search puzzle. They will go left to right or down.

S	A	Y	S	L	I	F	E	A	T	M
K	I	N	D	L	I	V	E	S	H	I
A	X	B	A	D	B	I	B	L	E	S
N	D	I	R	E	C	T	I	O	N	S
O	A	X	K	N	O	C	K	T	O	P
T	R	U	N	H	A	P	P	Y	N	E
H	K	N	E	E	D	T	U	R	N	C
E	W	E	S	T	U	M	B	L	E	I
R	U	S	S	H	O	W	I	N	G	A
L	I	G	H	T	S	I	N	F	U	L
S	O	M	E	T	H	I	N	G	D	O

dark	stumble	special	knock
directions	something	live	need
miss	turn	lot	on
unhappy	light	do	Bible
as	another	says	kind
showing	darkness	us	bad
the	sinful	happy	we
life			

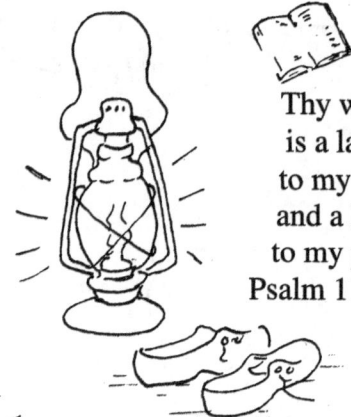

Thy word is a lamp to my feet and a light to my path. Psalm 119:105

This is one kind of lamp used before there was electricity. It burns a kind of oil called kerosene. A few people still use kerosene lamps.

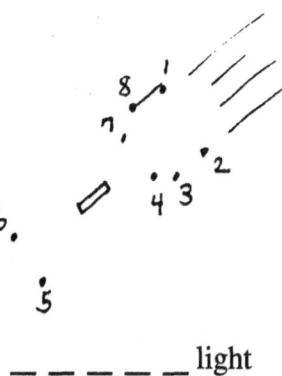

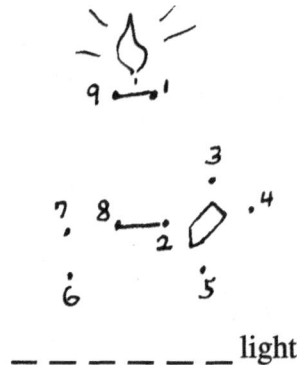

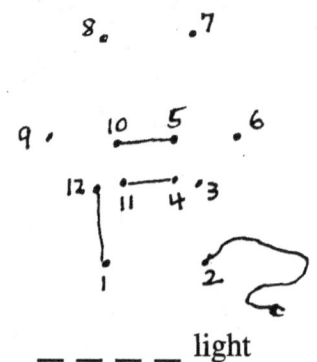

_ _ _ _ _ light

_ _ _ _ _ _ light

_ _ _ _ light

Can you name these other kinds of lights?

26

**Flowers fade but God's
word will stand forever.**

God's word is alive and active. It does things.
Read the sentences below. Cross out the things God's word does not do.
God's word —

helps change people's lives from bad to good.
cooks dinner.
tells us of God's love for all.
does laundry.
tells us to be sorry when we've done something wrong.
tells us God will forgive us.
cleans our room.
tells us to trust Jesus as our Savior.
shows us the way to live a happy life.
takes us to a ball game.
tells us God has prepared a place for us in heaven.
comforts us or makes us feel better when we are sad.
lives forever and will not fade away.

Find the words from the list in the word search puzzle. They will go left to right or down.

C	F	C	H	A	N	G	E	L	X	F
O	O	D	L	I	V	E	S	O	J	O
M	R	E	X	W	X	N	E	V	E	R
F	E	P	R	O	M	I	S	E	S	G
O	V	E	P	R	O	H	O	S	U	I
R	E	N	L	D	N	E	X	S	S	V
T	R	D	A	S	T	A	N	D	H	E
S	X	A	C	T	I	V	E	Y	O	C
F	A	D	E	S	T	E	X	O	P	A
I	T	L	I	V	I	N	G	U	E	N
I	T	T	R	U	S	T	K	E	E	P

word   Jesus
living   never
active   fades
change   stand
lives   forever
comforts   keep
loves   promises
hope   you
forgive   can
place   depend
heaven   on (2 times)
trust   it (3 times)

The grass withers, the flower fades: but the word of our God will stand forever.

— Isaiah 40:8

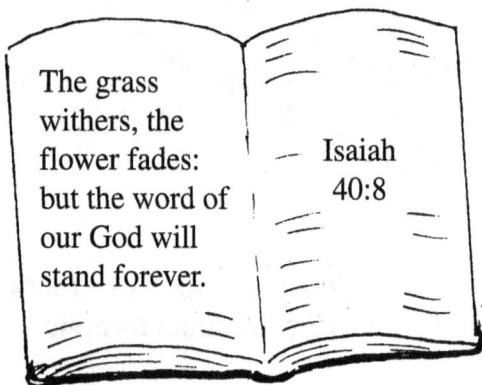

Use the words from Isaiah 40:8 to work the crossword puzzle.

Down
1. to remain unchanged
2. something that blooms

Across
2. something a flower does
3. something God has said
4. how long will God's word last?

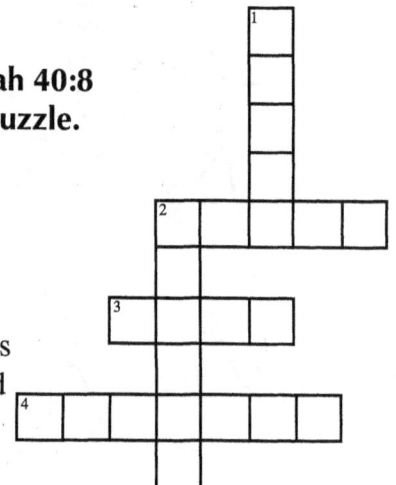

**Jesus the Word became a person like us,
showing us God's love and how he wants us to live.**

Choose the right word to fill in the blanks of these sentences.

Jesus the Word is _ _ _ _ _.

Jesus the Word is a _ _ _ _ _ _ _ _ _ _ to build our lives on.

Jesus the Word is the _ _ _ to go on the path of life.

Jesus the Word in our hearts will _ _ _ _ _ _ _ good things.

Jesus the Word _ _ _ _ _ us how we need to do better.

Jesus the Word gives _ _ _ _ _ to help us escape the bad things of life.

Jesus the Word is _ _ _ _ _ and active and will _ _ _ _ _ end.

Jesus the Word became a _ _ _ _ _ _ like us to bring us God's message of love.

person

real

foundation

way

never

alive

shows

light

produce

Find the underlined words from John 1:14 in the word search puzzle.
They will go left to right or down.

T	H	A	V	E	B	X	O	F
H	F	A	T	H	E	R	S	U
E	L	G	R	A	C	E	O	L
W	E	L	U	G	A	X	N	L
O	S	O	T	A	M	O	N	G
R	H	R	H	S	E	E	N	U
D	I	Y	L	I	V	E	D	S
E	S	O	N	L	Y	X	W	E

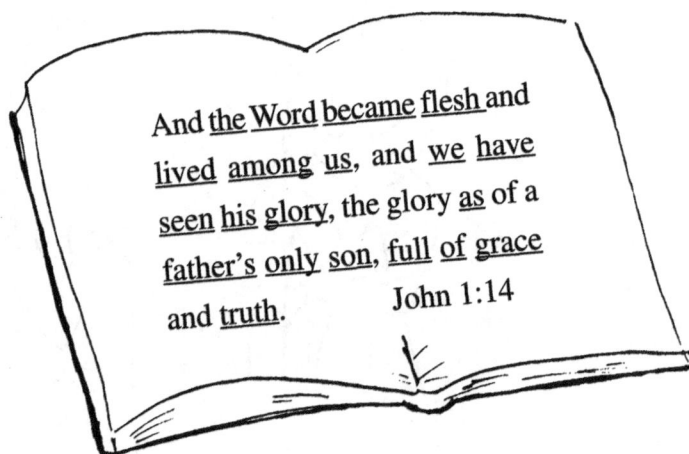

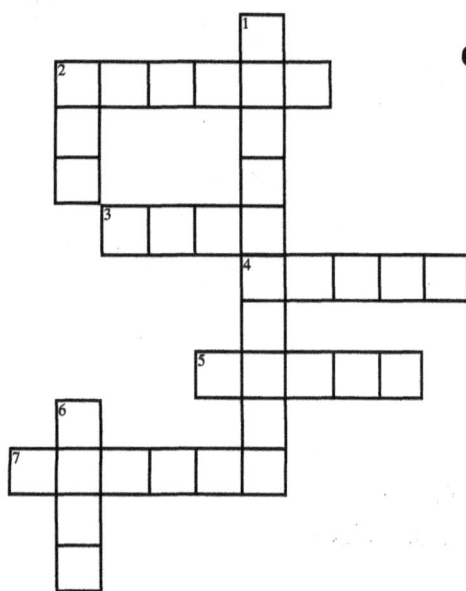

And the Word became flesh and lived among us, and we have seen his glory, the glory as of a father's only son, full of grace and truth. John 1:14

Can you work the crossword puzzle?

Down

1. Something to build on is a _____.
2. A _____ tells what road to take.
6. The Bible is _____, not made-up.

Across

2. We see ourselves in a _____.
3. We plant _____ for a crop.
4. Jesus the Word is _____.
5. When it's dark we need a _____.
7. God's word became a _____ in Jesus.

30

ANSWER KEYS

Pages 16, 18

Page 16

Use the list of words below to fill in the blanks.

Some stories are **f i c t i o n**. That means they didn't really happen. They are make-believe. Some stories are **f a c t**. That means they are true. The **s t o r i e s** and lessons in the Bible are true.

The word *Bible* comes from a Latin word. It **m e a n s** "little books." There are 66 **b o o k s** in our Bible. The Bible is also called Scripture or the Word of God. Earliest Scripture was written on animal **s k i n** or papyrus and made into rolls called **s c r o l l s**. Today we have printing presses, computers, and copiers to use.

Kings, prophets, fishermen, farmers, physicians, and missionaries were **s o m e** of those who were **g u i d e d** by God's Holy Spirit to write. It took over 1,000 **y e a r s** for the Bible to be completed. Only with God's guidance **c o u l d** such a book be written by so **m a n y** people and **f i t** together so well.

Through the years some have **t r i e d** to destroy the Bible. Others have **d i e d** to preserve it. In some countries it has been against the **l a w** to own or **p r i n t** a Bible. To people in those countries, the Bible is **v e r y** precious. It should be **p r e c i o u s** to **u s** too. We should **r e a d** from it each day.

Find words from the list in this word search puzzle. They will go down or left to right.

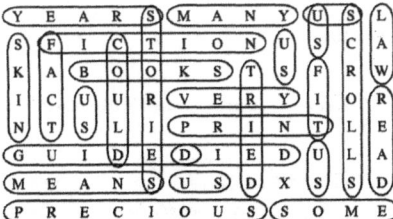

fiction	could
means	tried
scrolls	print
years	read
fit	stories
law	skin
precious	guided
fact	many
books	died
some	very
us (6 times in word search)	

All scripture is inspired by God ...
2 Timothy 3:16a

16

Page 18

Jesus <u>said</u> if we are <u>wise</u> and want a <u>strong</u>, <u>happy</u> <u>life</u>, we need to <u>listen</u> and <u>do</u> <u>what</u> he said. We will be like a <u>house</u> <u>built</u> on <u>rock</u>.

Jesus said <u>that</u> if we do <u>not</u> listen and do as he says, we are like a <u>foolish</u> <u>person</u> who built a house on <u>sand</u>. A <u>storm</u> <u>destroyed</u> that house.

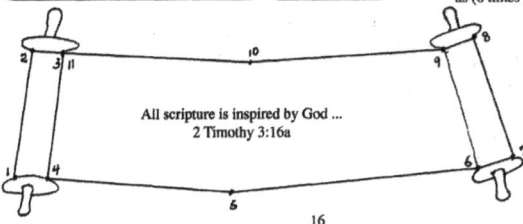

Find the underlined words in the word search puzzle. They will go left to right or down.

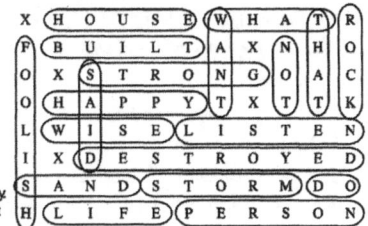

Here are some words from today's story. Draw a line from each word to what it means.

wise — to show good judgment
strong — a large mass of stone; a firm support
happy — to have joy and be glad
listen — to hear and to take advice
do — to perform or complete
built — to put together;
rock — loose, small grains of rock
foolish — to be silly, unwise, or stupid
sand —
storm — strong wind with rain, thunder and lightning, or snow
destroyed — to ruin, spoil, tear down, or put an end to
— to be powerful; to have special ability

Help this family move to their new house built on a strong foundation.

18

31

ANSWER KEYS

Pages 20, 22, 24

Unscramble the words, then find them in the word search puzzle below.

When we take a trip, maps show us the way to **go** (og). We must take the right **road** (odra) to get where we want. **Maps** (apMs) also tell interesting things about where we **are** (rea) going and places along the way to help us **enjoy** (yojen) our **trip** (iprt). The Bible says that living our **life** (feil) is like a journey. If living life is like a **journey** (neyurjo) along a **path** (thpa), then the Bible is like a map. The **Bible** (Bbeli) tells us the way to go. It **tells** (llets) us Jesus is the way. So we **must** (ustm) start off trusting Jesus. Then the Bible is like a map giving directions. Jesus helps us understand and **follow** (oowllf) the **directions** (rectsnoidi). We must trust Jesus and follow the directions or we'll never **get** (etg) **there** (ereht). Where? To heaven, of course. We all want to go to **heaven** (veeahn), but we want a happy life, a **happy** (pphay) journey as we go.

Word search:
```
G F X B  P A T H  X  R G M
E O       D I R E C T I O N S
T L G B   E N J O Y   A A L
M L O L   M T R I P   D R I
U O H     H E A V E N G A E F
S W       H A P P Y T H E R E
T E L L S J O U R N E Y
```

Use words from Proverbs 15:24 to fill in the squares of this puzzle.

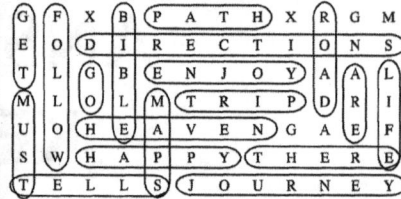

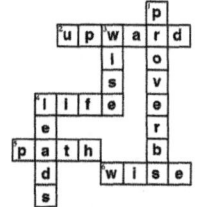

Crossword:
```
            p
u p w a r d r
      s    o
   l i f e  v
   e        e
p a t h     r
   d        b
   s      w i s e
```

For the wise the path of life leads upward.
Proverbs 15:24

Down
1. Proverbs
3. wise
4. leads

Across
2. upward
4. life
5. path
6. wise

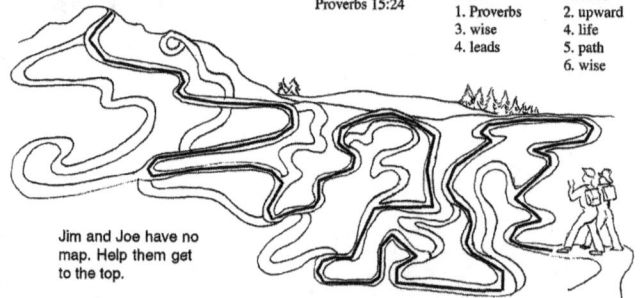

Jim and Joe have no map. Help them get to the top.

20

Use the list of words to fill in the blanks.

Jesus told some parables. A **parable** is a story about things everyone **knows** about. It helps us **understand** what God means. Jesus told a parable about **planting** seeds. When seeds fell on the path, **birds** ate them. The seeds on rocky ground had no **roots**. Some seed fell among **thorns** and the plants were **crowded** out. Some **seed** fell on good **soil** and they grew and produced **grain**. The seed stands for God's **word**. The soil stands for our **heart**. The seed eaten by birds stands for God's word in hearts that do not **believe**. The seed on rocky ground stands for God's word in hearts that at first believe but do **not** keep on. The seed in thorny **ground** stands for God's word in hearts that let other things be more important and God's word gets crowded out. The seed in **good** soil stands for God's word in hearts that believe and **do** what his word says. The good seed of God's word will produce a good life. Hearing and doing what God asks gives us happy things like **love**, **joy**, and peace.

Word list:
parable
understand
roots
soil
heart
ground
love
knows
planting
seed
grain
believe
good
birds
crowded
word
not
thorns
do (3 times in puzzle)
joy (3 times in puzzle)

Find the words from the list in the puzzle. They will go left to right or down.

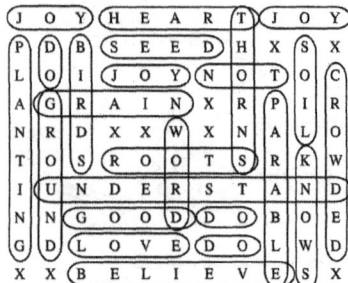

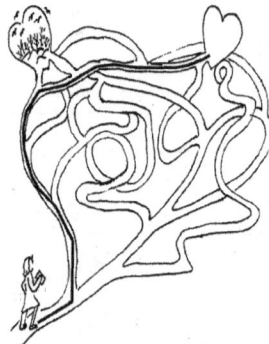

Word search:
```
J O Y  H E A R T  J O Y
P D B  S E E D  H X S X
L O I  J O Y  N O T O C
A G R A I N  X R P I R
N R D X X W X N A L O
T O S  R O O T S  R R W
I U N D E R S T A N D
N G O O D D D O B O E
G D L O V E D O L W D
X X B E L I E V E S X
```

Help Sue with her Bible find her way to the heart that has no birds, rocks, or thorns.

22

Find the underlined words in the word search puzzle. They will go left to right or down.

We **look** in a **mirror** and see **ourselves**. Our **face** is **dirty** and our **hair** is **messy**. So we **wash** our face and **comb** our hair. It would be **silly** to **see** what we **need** and just go **away** **not** doing **anything** about it.

The Bible is like a mirror. We **read** the Bible or **hear** it **taught** and we see how **we** need to do **better**. We need to **do** what God's **word** says. Then we will be **blessed** or **made** happy. What are some **things** you need to do better?

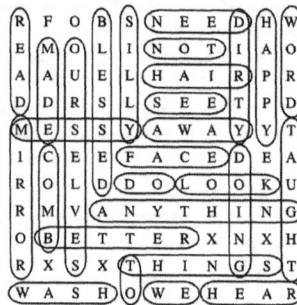

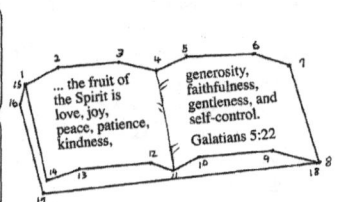

Word search:
```
R F O B S  N E E D H W
E A M O L I  N O T  A O
A U U R S L L  H A I R P R
D D R S L L  S E E T  D
M E S S Y  A W A Y  E A
I C E E  F A C E D  E U
R O L D  D O L O O K  G
R M V  A N Y T H I N G
O B E T T E R X N X H
R X S X  T H I N G S T
W A S H O W E H E A R
```

... the fruit of the Spirit is love, joy, peace, patience, kindness,

generosity, faithfulness, gentleness, and self-control.
Galatians 5:22

When we look in the Bible at Galatians 5:22, we see some things we need to do better. Draw a line to the words that will finish the sentence.

I show love when I want good t... → do as he asks.
I show joy when I s... → things for others.
I show peace when I try to g... → refuse to argue or get angry.
I show patience when I obey w... → smile.
I show kindness when I o... → am careful not to hurt anyone.
I show generosity when I s... → share.
I show faithfulness when I k... → offer to help Mom with chores.
I show gentleness when I a... → without complaining.
I show self-control when I r... → get along with others.
I show love for Jesus when I d... → keep my promises.

24

ANSWER KEYS

Pages 26, 28, 30

Fill in the missing words. Use the pictures to help.

When the **s u n** goes down, it is dark. If it is dark, we might stumble or **f a l l** or knock something over. We need to turn on a **l i g h t**. The Bible talks about another kind of darkness. The Bible calls bad, sinful, **u n h a p p y** things darkness. For this kind of darkness we need a special kind of light. God's word is that special **l i g h t**. God's word gives us directions on how to live and how to miss a lot of bad, sinful, unhappy things. We need to do as God's word says. It is like a light showing us the way to live a happy life.

Find the words from the list in the word search puzzle. They will go left to right or down.

```
S A Y S  L I F E  A T M
K I N D  L I V E  A S H I
A X B A D  B I B L E  S
N D I R E C T I O N S  S
O A X K N O C K T O P  E
T K R U N H A P P Y N  N
H E N E E D T U R N C  I
E W E S T U M B L E I
R U S S H O W I N G A
L I G H T S I N F U L
S O M E T H I N G D O
```

dark	stumble	special	knock
directions	something	live	need
miss	turn	lot	on
unhappy	light	do	Bible
as	another	says	kind
showing	darkness	us	bad
the	sinful	happy	we
life			

Thy word
is a lamp
to my feet
and a light
to my path.
Psalm 119:105

This is one kind of lamp used before there was electricity. It burns a kind of oil called kerosene. A few people still use kerosene lamps.

f l a s h light   **c a n d l e** light   **l a m p** light

Can you name these other kinds of lights?

26

God's word is alive and active. It does things.
Read the sentences below. Cross out the things God's word does not do.

God's word —

helps change people's lives from bad to good.
~~cooks dinner.~~
tells us of God's love for all.
~~does laundry.~~
tells us to be sorry when we've done something wrong.
tells us God will forgive us.
~~cleans our room.~~
tells us to trust Jesus as our Savior.
shows us the way to live a happy life.
~~takes us to a ball game.~~
tells us God has prepared a place for us in heaven.
comforts us or makes us feel better when we are sad.
lives forever and will not fade away.

Find the words from the list in the word search puzzle. They will go left to right or down.

```
C F C H A N G E L X F
O O D L I V E S O J O
M R E X W X N E V E R
F E P R O M I S E S G
O V E P R O H O S U I
R E N L D E N X I V
T R D A S T A N D H E
S X A C T I V E Y O C
F A D E S T E X O P A
I T L I V I N G U E N
I T T R U S T K E E P
```

word	Jesus
living	never
active	fades
change	stand
lives	forever
comforts	keep
loves	promises
hope	you
forgive	can
place	depend
heaven	on (2 times)
trust	it (3 times)

The grass withers, the flower fades: but the word of our God will stand forever.
Isaiah 40:8

Use the words from Isaiah 40:8 to work the crossword puzzle.

Down
1. to remain unchanged
2. something that blooms

Across
2. something a flower does
3. something God has said
4. how long will God's word last?

```
        s
        t
        a
        n
      f a d e s
        w o r d
        o w
    f o r e v e r
        r
```

28

Choose the right word to fill in the blanks of these sentences.

Jesus the Word is **r e a l**.
Jesus the Word is a **f o u n d a t i o n** to build our lives on.
Jesus the Word is the **w a y** to go on the path of life.
Jesus the Word in our hearts will **p r o d u c e** good things.
Jesus the Word **s h o w s** us how we need to do better.
Jesus the Word gives **l i g h t** to help us escape the bad things of life.
Jesus the Word is **a l i v e** and active and will **n e v e r** end.
Jesus the Word became a **p e r s o n** like us to bring us God's message of love.

person
real
foundation
way
never
alive
shows
light
produce

Find the underlined words from John 1:14 in the word search puzzle. They will go left to right or down.

```
T H A V E B X O F
H F A T H E R S U L
E L G R A C E O L
W E L U G A X N
O S O T A M O N G
R H R H S E E N U
D I Y L I V E D S
E S O N L Y X W E
```

And the Word became flesh and lived among us, and we have seen his glory, the glory as of a father's only son, full of grace and truth.
John 1:14

Can you work the crossword puzzle?

```
        f
  m i r r o r
  a     u
  p   s e e d
        a l i v e
        t
      l i g h t
  r     o
p e r s o n
  a
  l
```

Down
1. Something to build on is a **foundation**.
2. A **map** tells what road to take.
6. The Bible is **real**, not made-up.

Across
2. We see ourselves in a **mirror**.
3. We plant **seed** for a crop.
4. Jesus the Word is **alive**.
5. When it's dark we need a **light**.
7. God's word became a **person** in Jesus.

30

33

3

And everyone who hears these words of mine and does not act on them will be like a foolish man who built his house on sand.

4

The rain fell, and the floods came, and the winds blew and beat against that house, and it fell — and great was its fall!"

— Matthew 7:24-27

"Everyone then who hears these words of mine and acts on them will be like a wise man who built his house on rock.

1

The rain fell, the floods came, and the winds blew and beat on that house, but it did not fall because it had been founded on rock.

2

Other seeds fell on good soil and brought forth grain....

Other seeds fell among thorns, and the thorns grew up and choked them.

Other seeds fell on rocky ground ... and since they had no root, they withered away.

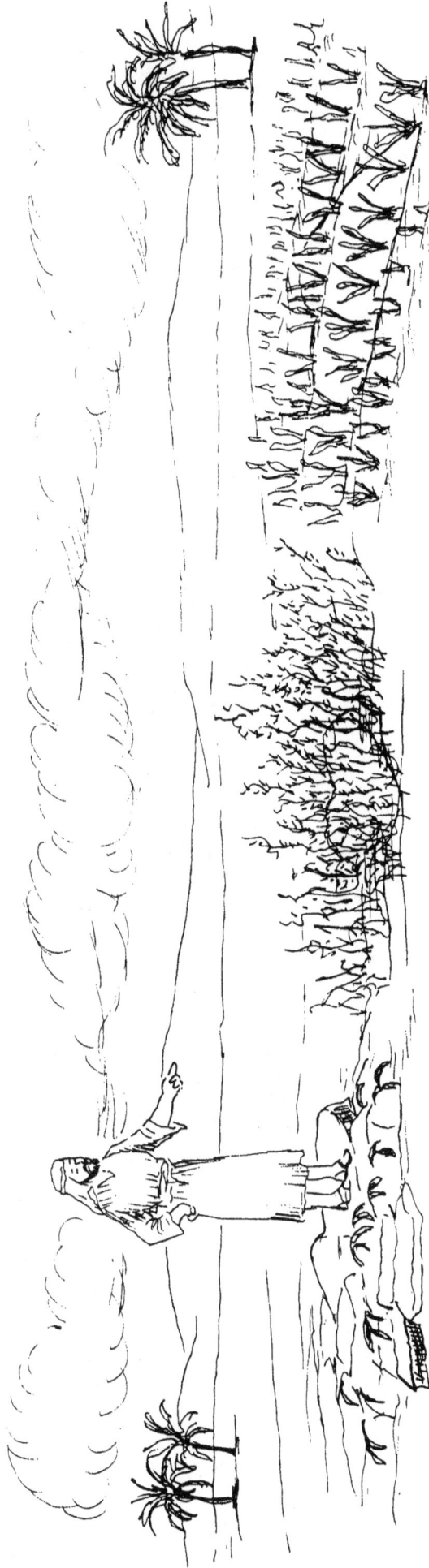

LOVE

KINDNESS

GENEROSITY

FAITHFULNESS

GALATIONS 5:22

GENTLENESS

SELF-CONTROL

PATIENCE

PEACE

JOY

But as for what was sown on good soil, this is the one who hears the word and understands it, who indeed bears fruit.

— Matthew 13:3-8, 18-23

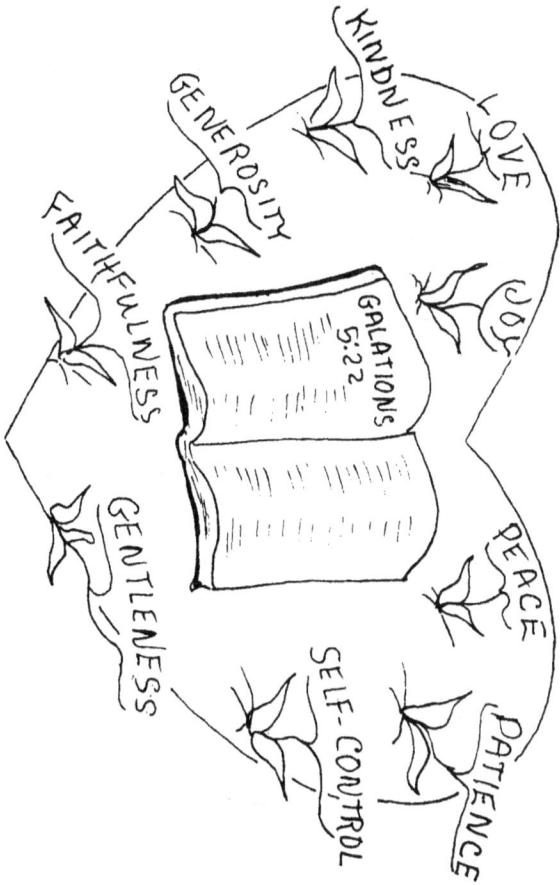

4

Some seeds fell on the path, and the birds came and ate them up.

www.ingramcontent.com/pod-product-compliance
Lightning Source LLC
LaVergne TN
LVHW061342060426
835511LV00014B/2063